Where do they Grow?

by Lynne Rickards

CAMBRIDGE UNIVERSITY PRESS

UCL Institute of Education

Where do oranges grow?

Oranges grow on a tree.

3

Where do potatoes grow?

Potatoes grow in the ground.

Where do bananas grow?

Bananas grow on a tree.

Where do carrots grow?

Carrots grow in the ground.

Where do apples grow?

Apples grow on a tree.

Where do onions grow?

Onions grow in the ground.

13

Where do olives grow?

Olives grow on a tree.

Where do they Grow? ● Lynne Rickards

Teaching notes written by Sue Bodman and Glen Franklin

Using this book

Developing reading comprehension

This non-fiction report uses a question and answer structure to present where some commonly-used fruit and vegetables grow. The two structures are used repetitively throughout the book. Children who live in cities and towns may not see food being grown. In this instance, discuss how the fruit and vegetables we eat are grown and that they may grow on trees or bushes in the ground.

Grammar and sentence structure

- Text is well-spaced to support the development of one-to-one correspondence.

- Two lines of text on each page support the reinforcement of return sweep whilst tracking a slightly longer text.

- In contexts where children are learning English as an additional language, support by rehearsing the sentence structure orally before introducing the book.

Word meaning and spelling

- The prepositions ('on', 'in') change depending on the context of each page.

- The nouns are used with lower case and capital letters, depending on their position in the sentence.

Curriculum links

Mathematics – Use pictures of fruit and vegetables to sort into sets according to where they grow.

Science – Cress, beansprouts and lentils can be grown in the classroom. This could lead to investigations. What do they need to grow? Light? Water? Where in the classroom do they grow best?

Learning Outcomes

Children can:

- understand that print carries meaning and is read from left to right, top to bottom

- use initial letter information to check word choice

- use picture information and known letters to inform reading for the precise meaning and to discriminate between 'in' and 'on'

- track two lines of simple repetitive text.

A guided reading lesson

Book Introduction

Give a book to each child and read the title.

Orientation

Give a brief orientation to the text: *This book will tell us about where the food that we eat grows.*

Preparation

Cover: Ask the children to locate the word 'Where' using their fingers as 'frames'. How did they know which word was 'Where'? Could they use the letter information to locate it on every page.

Page 2: Introduce the question structure by saying, *The book asks 'Where do oranges grow?' It asks a question. I use my voice to sound like a question.* Repeat the question a few times with a question intonation and ask the children to practise that too. Then say, *Read the question to yourself and point carefully to each word as you do.* Check that the children are able to track to each word accurately and support if this is challenging. Say: *Well done. Make sure you point to each word when you read by yourself.*

So let's look at the picture to see if we can answer the question. Where do oranges grow? Yes, that's right – they grow on a tree. Find the words 'on a tree'. Well done, you were looking at the letters to find the words.

Page 4. Say: *Where do potatoes grow? Not on a tree. Yes, in the ground. Find the word 'in the ground'. Well done again. You were looking at the letters to find 'in the ground'. So how can we check if the other fruit and vegetables in this book grow 'on a tree' or 'in the ground'? Yes, we can do two things. We can look at the picture and we can look at the letters to help us.*

Strategy Check

Prepare the children for checking one-to-one correspondence as they read independently. Say: *Point to each word with your finger as you read*